Quilt of Life

Kathryn A. Virnig

If a quilt represented your life,

with each square representing a person you have

Touched, Loved or

Who loved you

When your life ended,

what would your Quilt of Life look like?

PUBLISHER'S ACKNOWLEDGMENT

The publisher wishes to acknowledge all the wonderful people who contributed their time, talents and support during the creation of this book. I have been touched by your generosity and kindness. Each of you has become a part of my Quilt of Life.

A portion of the proceeds from the sale of this book will benefit Victoria's Quilts©, a non-profit organization dedicated to supplying hand-made quilts to cancer patients and to cancer treatment facilities. www.victoriasquilts.com

Copyright © 2002 Kathryn A. Virnig
Published by
Lily Field Publishing
P.O. Box 391
New Ulm, MN 56073
Printed in the United States of America
ISBN 0-9726164-0-3
Photography & Graphic Design by Carrie Forstner

What does it look like today?

Remembering no quilt is made up of

Possessions,

Wealth

or

Fame

Only People

Would it be a single square,

isolated from the world?

A quilt of one color,

not letting anyone who wasn't like you into

the Fabric of your Quilt?

Would all your pieces be the same size?

Would a pattern emerge?

Or would it be a Mosaic of colors,

a Tapestry to be displayed?

Life is made of many choices and paths.

So many people that enter in every day

You choose to let them in,

or you let them pass you by.

Similar to a quilt maker

choosing every

Fabric,
Shape and Size.

In my time, I have seen many

Quilts of Life.

Some that are Inspiring

Others Despairing

Some that are sewn together only with

Threads of Gold

Others that are

made of

Steel

Including my own ever changing

Quilt of Life.

But to this day, the most beautiful

Quilt of Life

I have ever seen is that of my

Mother.

In the center of her quilt she placed her Family,

her most prized possession.

Sewn together patiently with the strongest

Threads of Faith

Their pieces came in many shapes, sizes and textures, colors bright and bold.

Though she loved them individually,

she treasured them as a whole.

Their bond was everlasting.

Tied with love and friendship,

Laughter and Pain,

Joining each together with unending devotion.

She did not limit her quilt to only family.

She welcomed everyone to join the cloth,

Rich, Poor,

Young and Old,

the Strong

and the Weak.

Some joined who were not whole,

they were Frayed at the edges, scared and alone.

Some had torn away from other Quilts,

or had no quilt of their own.

This did not matter to her.

She would take her quilt, her life,

and wrap it around them,

giving them Shelter from the storm.

She would teach them how to make their own quilts

Sewn with Faith and Love.

Her life was not charmed,

for she knew sorrow and pain,

hard work and disappointment.

During these difficult times she knew what to do.

She would use her quilt to lift her spirits,

Holding it close gave her

Strength,

Courage

and Faith.

It kept her Safe and Warm.

Sometimes pieces of her own quilt came undone,

with the threads pulling away

taking other pieces with them.

Patiently she would pull them back together,

Tenderly mending them with

Prayer and Kindness

Compassion and Humanity.

When people saw her quilt and its beauty

they also wanted to join the Fabric.

And it grew in color and splendor.

It was not square or round.

No pattern emerged,

but a multitude of lives touched by one person.

It was an amazing sight to see,

Rich with

Color and *Texture*.

So as you walk on your path of life,

and journey through this world,

Remember . . .

You are the Quilt Maker.

You are the one who can touch the lives

of people around you.

Make your quilt as

Large,

Colorful

and Beautiful

as you can.

I am proud to say that I was a part of my

Mother's

Quilt of Life.

*I*t has shown me and many others that it is not the

things you have that make you rich,

it is the people you touch and the ones that touch you.

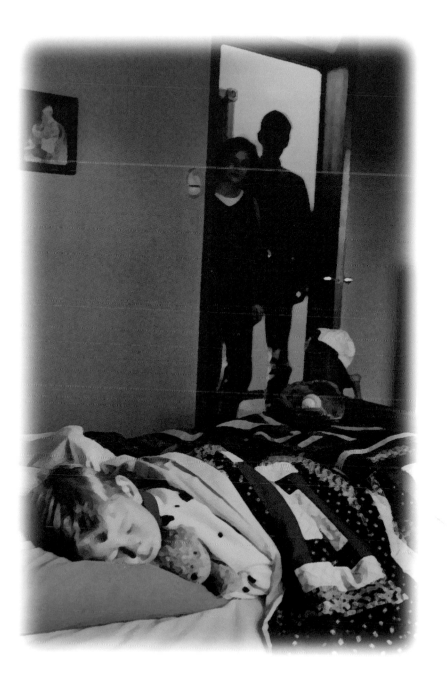

And when you look at this simple piece of fabric,

tell yourself you will make a *Difference*

in just one person's life.

And let the

Tapestry of your Life

Unfold.

Lily Field Publishing